Without Passport
or Apology

Without Passport or Apology
Ishaq Imruh Bakari

Smokestack Books
1 Lake Terrace, Grewelthorpe, Ripon HG4 3BU
e-mail: info@smokestack-books.co.uk
www.smokestack-books.co.uk

Text copyright 2017,
Ishaq Imruh Bakari,
all rights reserved.

ISBN 978-0-9955635-4-4

Smokestack Books is represented
by Inpress Ltd

for Ameerah

Contents

In Search of the Ceremonies
The Awakening	13
There Was Once a Young Boy	14
Marcus Garvey Stood on Basseterre Bay Road	16
Mister Farrakhan and the Steelband	19
Haiti is Once Again…	21
Signs And Fragments	25
Wild Fires at the End of a Summer	27
So…Where Did You Come From?	30
The Battle of Paris 2005	33
Sipping Tea at the Queen's Jubilee	35
The Miracle of Kibera	38
Mzee, Until Finally… Until Later!	39
Qunu Welcomes You	41
Diaspora Dialogic	42
In the House of Legends	44
Today is Special	47

Dr Livingstone's Casebook
Housing Problems	51
Robbery	53
Retaking Buchanan	54
Tears and Laughter Embrace in the Blood-Stained Forest	57
Paper Clips are Precious in Rwanda	63
Tangled Melodies	65
Juffure in the Tourist Season	72
Jane	73
Arriving at Bagamoyo	75
Dr. Livingstone, We Know	76
Bagamoyo Smile	78
The End of Slavery in Zanzibar	80
The Sultan's Ruins	81
Salme's Night Flight	82
Death of a Neem Tree	83
After the Rain	85
Starehe – Nafsi Poa	88
The Border	90

Digging Down
Taking the Medicine	95
The Journey	98
Dreamworker	101
Kaieteur Callaloo	102
Small Island Pride	103
Approaching the Savannah from the Middle Passage	105
Tongues: Drum Sounds and Firewood	106
Pasero	108
Heritage	110
Abstract	111
Monk's Mood	115
Eyes	116
Travelling Miles With You	117
Desert Flower	119
The Rose	121
Boomerang	122
Send Me a Bouquet of Bones	123

Interludes
Requiem for the Widow of a Colonial Jumbie	127
In the Story So Far	135
From a Long Line of Soldiers	140

One Season of Voyages
Departure-Distance-Destination	145
Nationals-Returning Residents-Aliens	147
The Marketplace	149
The Will to Walk	151
Zawadi Ya Zenj/A Gift of Zanzibar	152
Ferry Crossing	153
Askari	154
Arusha	155
Treasures	156

Notes	159
Acknowledgements	161

In Search of
the Ceremonies

The Awakening

Too much clutter
here the old world
intrudes pushing
and squeezing
into spaces alien
to its geometry

New forms and simplicity
have split the rock of habit
stubborn and commanding

Light takes root where
weeds of past returnings
scramble for balance

Too much clutter
here quicksand turns
in the dawn
there is sunset
in the infinite void
volcanoes weep

There Was Once a Young Boy

There was once
a young boy
who often stood
as far out to sea
as the island's jetty
would permit

some fifty yards away
from his home shore
where the sea bottom
could still be seen
through clear water
on a day when no tourist boat
or man-o-war had muddied the calm tide
bringing slanted smiles and crooked eyes
pleasure seekers and promises
no better than a pretty fish hook

There was once
a young boy
who often looked
far out to sea knowing
that the island's geography
was a fraud

since its discovery
departing boats
except by force of a squall
would not go over
the horizon wall
but take a passage out of sight
behind the island facing
away from the government
school books seeking a route
to a more desirable disembarkation

There was once
a young boy
who learnt to see
around corners and sing
the moments muzzled
by the road-march ramajay

Marcus Garvey Stood on Basseterre Bay Road

As with all comings
many would have claimed
to have seen the signs   time
                                          was already ticking
                                          blood
                                          was already boiling

messages had passed between
labourers and factory workers
potent songs were sung
by barefoot travellers and proud women   serving at high tables

The circus clock
was standing still
and going nowhere   when Marcus Garvey
                                          stood on Basseterre Bay Road
                                          not far from the old slave
                                          market in Pall Mall Square

His voice took the sea
breeze inland
where volcanic rock resides

He stood to speak
of citizens
He stood to speak
of hope

He stood to speak
of self-confidence
He stood to speak
of free will

He stood to speak
of duty and responsibility
He stood to speak
of self-expression and liberty

    he spoke
    of the ungodliness
    that is inequality

here I stand
he said
because of my purpose

    he spoke
    of the devil
    that is illiteracy

determined to leave
a mark more permanent
than the smell of fried fish

    he spoke
    of the hell
    that is misery

the Mutual Improvement Society
Hall was packed
with the capacity for greatness

    he spoke
    of the prison
    that is poverty

Nineteen thirty-seven
was a good year for cane fires
and better was supposed to come

Sharp machetes
had already
cleared a path

    from Jamaica to Ethiopia
    to the Cape and Cairo
    across Harlem to raise
    a flicker on Kilimanjaro

Among the gathered
where injustice had been
a constant visitor
and torn-up caps no shield
from torture
the black-star flag fluttered

But when Marcus Garvey stood
on Basseterre Bay Road   he knew
                                      there was much more
                                      work to do

Threadbare after   years of treachery
his words still rattled the circus clock
echoing across   the slave market tombs
holding the blood-stained auction block

Like the sea breeze
that is always sure   to become a hurricane
the weary rocked
on the wing of Marcus   Garvey's refrain

                                      fix-up you'self
                                      fix-up you'self
                                      fix-up you'self

Mister Farrakhan and the Steelband

Yes mi frien'
the honourable brother
come home again...

No need for appointment
just passing by
the door is always open
just dropping in

Yes mi frien'
the honourable brother
come home again...

In this age
when nations
have no borders
ancestral roots
criss-cross the gateways
the sea-lanes
and the cyber-ways
that offer liberty

Yes mi frien'
coming home is all
part of the story

The honourable brother
is a celebrity
and notoriety is always good
for a photo opportunity but in the carnival cavalcade
everyone is a masquerade

He steps between
the clapping
and the stillness of memory

There he finds
a seat waiting
with the warmth of familiarity

So he sits around the gathered
fire of ancient tongues
he wipes the sweat from his brow
and reaches out beyond
the unforeseen circumstances
and the clunk of rusty chains

It is a message
heard through landscapes
where dollar exchange prevails

It is an interruption
in a season of goat-head smiles
where home is a house for sale

It is a message heard
like a txt or a tweet
leaning tired
at the corner of a street

So jam if you jamming
whine if you whining
but please no serious talking
make room for the tourist boat coming   in the carnival cavalcade
                                                                    everyone is a masquerade

Haiti is Once Again…

History does not
repeat itself   it hangs

Around the neck
like a stone   or a talisman

And now within
the moment that it takes
a guillotine
to settle a score

And now beneath
the rubble of our
window dressing
the cries of orphans choke

Haiti is once again
the hurt   in the soul
the amputation   that never healed
the torch   flame of cane fires
Haiti is once again…

The clocks have stopped
face and arms
lay unidentified
where they stood

The laughter remembered
hangs on a limping
stride amidst the silence
in abundant after-shock

The tears flow
where no water
can be found

it burns in the steam
It stains and seeps
from ragged thoughts
that yearn for maps
to the neighbourhood streets

Haiti is once again...

Somewhere in a museum
it will be recalled

Somewhere the crimes
of Napoleonic brotherhood

Somewhere the compromises
of the new Americas

Somewhere it will
be condemned
to its loneliness beyond
the age of enlightenment

Somewhere the architects
of banana republics

Somewhere the tyrannies
that censure liberty

Haiti is once again...

At the turn of a new century
it is the twelfth of January
and the world is looking
the other way

    It is a normal day   with business and its intrigues
                                              aid and its debt relief
                                              arms dealers and their wars

                    good causes and their epidemics

It was a normal day   in Cité Soleil
                                  and Jacmel
                                  in Port-au-Prince no doubt
                                  at the Citadel

And the world was looking
the other way   until...

                                the interruption

                                the disruption

calamity so epic and severe
prophets were born
in deceit and complicity

and as the vibrations
settled into still life
lost words rolled off
the cliffs of corpses

the nameless
spoke their last
in epitaphs sealed in blood
dust and lost possessions

How much less
sure my staggering walk
How much less
certain my world stories

familiar finger prints
are being left
at the scenes of crime
in the aftermath

Haiti is once again
at the cross-roads

*In whose image
the zombification...?*

Haiti is once again
at the turn of a new century

*In whose image
the deification...?*

Haiti is once again
at the threshold
between bondage
and the ease of flight   in search of the ceremonies
                                                      of our healing....

Signs and Fragments

This picture

        takes away
        the best of you

This camera

        strip of light   grabbed by a raider
        in flight

Leaving what's left
without the rest of you

It takes away   the best of you

Return

        sweet embrace at morning
        after night

Return

        the wholeness of you
        without amputation
        or camouflage
        without broken melody   the best of you

        without   this middle
                                this centre
                                that is not whole
        without   this certainty
                                that has
                                no balance
        without   the showbiz
                                the lights
                                that keep darkness...

The lights that keep
darkness over the earth
Return the sight
to where blindness smiles
in one-eyed ecstasy

This picture

                        in the mirror
                        seen in stainless
                        stolen diamonds dancing
                        in the silent whirlpool
                        where pain and poise
                        are one for now!

No more

                        those flashing lights
                        meeting celebrities
                        on parade
                        the dreams in hand-baskets
                        and trolleys filled
                        with fragments of a shopping
                        list remembered
                        and reclaimed from a crash
                        landing...
                        a crash
                        ending...

When the demons   called to say

History is knocking   slowly knocking
                        filling in the gaps
                        and the empty gourds
                        that hung where
                        no rain fell

History is knocking   softly knocking
                        knowing where sand
                        castles crumble
                        new dirt tracks arise...

Wild Fires at the End of a Summer

I

The ecstasy of anger
infectious and intoxicating
gathered steam turning
the long summer day
into a royal visit of hyenas

It came riding the echo
of a casual gunshot
all in a day's work
for thugs who hide behind
designer swag and unmarked cars

Seeping from the toxic
roots of the green and pleasant land
riots returned
to the streets of London tearing
at the altars of consumer veneration

No leaders here among
the dry leaves of neighbourhood life
the tower block
is a playground too small
for the rage to mix and mashup

As postcode walls
tumbled into flames of rubble
and discarded junk
an ecstatic wave surged
across the summer nights

All things no more
than cheap must go
the brand names incinerated
with humpty dumpty and the straw
inside his head

The respectable public watched
but did not see the barking
choruses of imperial flag-bearers
providing sustenance and promise
for another rampage to the ever present

Like wild fires at the end of a summer
their sound-bites betrayed a winter
chill that will return
with ritual thrill to trade
with the legacy of plunder

II

Just enough time
to find her way home

The street map
was changing fast before her eyes

Just enough time
to make a last stand

The heroine of Hackney
raised a barricade to a simple truth

In her lone voice
against the maelstrom

An ancient call
to live beyond the cage of self-denial

In her lone voice
the frenzy of a noble rage

An ancient call
to rise beyond the flash of mirrors in the dark

So… Where Did You Come From?

So...   where did you
                                   come from

This face   not anchored
                                   in the right place

It is a kite dancing
without string
A signature shaped
in unusual size

Today I had
to meet
at this appointed time
the question
through gated smile
it came avoiding glances
but with interrogation
and verdict close to hand   so...
                             where did you
                             come from...

Today I had
to hear
a silence painted
by a tax man
who has waited life-long
patiently to collect
with shotgun and trinket
bag close to hand

At this moment
an urgent answer
is desired to determine
the baggage I bring
into the room
at this border post
not knowing where
in my journey   there is a pause
                          a comma or a paragraph
                          to disappear
                          as far back

Today
what do I say
precise words are not
enough for songs
not enough
for confessions
that cast a shadow
on this imperial earth

Today I saw
polite derision in smoke
rising from an expectation
shivering in an echo
brought back
after robbing graves
and I am arriving
from somewhere   not anchored
                          in a future place
                          sealed in certainty
                          as far back

Tell me I said
stepping on stones
to the echo
are you emperor or empress
a fashion statement no less
or another wonder of the world
are you belly of barracuda
or stolen mother of pearl

So... where did you
come from...

The Battle of Paris 2005

the boulevards are aflame
footsteps scattered
around the bohemian terraces
are conversing in sullen tones

Gentlemen,
do we protect the state(ment)
or do we toast
your liberal discretion

the vintage taste
returns to haunt
the tricolour charade

Liberté is banished

                                              to the mouldy camouflage
                                              where Sartre
                                              and Foucault promenade
                                              and stale baguettes
                                              are shipped out of town
                                              by poodle track

Fraternité is cannibalised

                                              bloating the gut brain
                                              where memory
                                              is the wretched
                                              smell of captives
                                              rotting at the foyers
                                              in Haiti's cesspool story

Egalité is stripped

                                              down to its bare elegance
                                              Pierre Cardin is now
                                              loose and hot
                                              with cravat ruffled
                                              like an eager noose
                                              soaked in winter red

Gentlemen,
if there are no more
questions there is work
to be done

no heroes here
no climax or crescendo
in the air

the answers surge
from armchairs
from the smoke that has come
to stay and anchor firm

this battle day
the answers linger
without promise

triumphant claims are parodies
without territorial space
islands of desolation
loom in the urban landscape

and a procession of rage
brings the Kasbah home

Sipping Tea at the Queen's Jubilee

I

My name is Dedan Kimathi
and I am here to sip tea
at the Queen's jubilee
we are good friends
as you will see

> *a few days late*
> *but what hell*
> *with funeral speed*
> *we both made for our destination*
> *across the dusty trophies*
> *seasoned in colonial affectation*

Her flotilla gathered steam
retracing Empire tracks
pinstriped and formal
it arrived on time official
in order and correct

The old wounds that I
bring are here seeping
from scrambled serenades
and the memories moulded
into resplendent treasures

II

My name is Dedan Kimathi
with noose around my neck
with trampled testimonies in hand
the old school boys on parade recall
route marches across my land

> *a few days late*
> *but what the hell*
> *as good friends*
> *please accept my apology*
> *still stuttering from the chill*
> *sealed by a state of emergency*

At intervals between
the ceremonies of delusion
we break for repartee
polite underskirts bring glee
to a nation is search of itself

The precision of the internment
ground is present all around
the smell of sulphur in the air
the church bells and gun
salutes are majestic in their flair

III

My name is Dedan Kimathi
and I am here as you can see
at the jubilee with you
there is more to share
than a thing or two

> *a few days late*
> *but what the hell*
> *we both arrive*
> *with the common dirt and wealth*
> *wrapped in the blue rot*
> *dust of dungeons built on stealth*

Today the head that holds
the crown must bear the weight
unfurled with callous might
to command a hero's right
and ordain genuflection

Today in the afternoon
shadow against the green glow
across the Nakuru highlands
in the silhouette I am the black
missing from the union jack

The Miracle of Kibera

Captured on camera
her defiance is iconic
watch her leap towards
another development goal

With a child strapped
to her back she steals
a moment meant for dying
in the circus of unfinished business

The sewage was ripe
after the rains had come and stayed

The news headlines were flooded
as secrets of the underbelly boiled

Resolute with raised
hands for wings
watch her straddle
the daily dollar-a-day

The silence in the child's eye
is searching for meaning that cannot
wait for the next candidate
his excellency is deferred

She will fly
because she must
stretch the milk inside her breast

She will fly because
there is no other way
out...

Mzee, Until Finally… Until Later!

for Mzee Godwin Kaduma

There is luggage
to be collected
with well shaped
words and dancing
choruses that bring light

There is luggage
to be collected
everywhere the fragments
in between the ruins
and the rain

And so the story is told
unfolding like a flower
Mzee, the way you
moved each stone
solidly into place
taking the time to build
where crumbling
will not visit

And so the story is told
laced with moonlight
and other mysteries
woven solid
against the changing
winds and the carelessness
that comes
with a hangover

And so the story is told
there are new emergencies
in voices persistent
as Bagamoyo's dirt roads
there are new summonses
worn calmly around shoulders
stern as the Iringa hill
…a refuge … a memory

Now we must sigh
as the bell sings
a slow march

Now we must sigh
as the stoic smile
offers gifts of fire

There is luggage
to be collected
with discerning touch
no flags or fickle
monuments of vanity

There is luggage
to be collected
for the worker bees
a job of sweet
vocation calls
enduring until …finally
…until later

Qunu Welcomes You

for Madiba

The questions lingered
before your eyes the years
and jagged rocks proclaimed
the treacherous route to freedom

Qunu…
welcomes you

The parables nesting
in bad dreams made maps
packaged in smoke signals
for the gentle journey home

Qunu…
welcomes you

There is a slow determined march
taking you to a distant tranquil place
where earth reclaimed
will savour the sight of birds

Qunu…
welcomes you

Diaspora Dialogic

for Stuart Hall

It is too late to wave
time has taken its pound
of flesh and the cushion
for soft landing

Cardboard box
belongings held high
above the ticking miles
the mean seams
and the hip
hop strut have left
a noisiness
dripping over
grey indifference

It is too late to wave
smoke signals hold
no memory of streets
paved with gold

He takes a bow
and leaves a hurricane
he leaves a smiling
fist shaking
scattered baggage
into shape
it is a new day now
for night dreams
of stepping razor cool

Post cards come
from post codes
where flash mobs squat
naked in broken banks
where everything is for sale
in photo-shop this wave
deferred is a parting salute
to what cannot be
but must exist

In the House of Legends

for Courtney Pine

Head held high above
this pirate's throne
this barren river
of glass beads
and broken mirrors   *here lies the clay pot handed*
                           down after a storm

Old litanies expire
to inspire the incendiary
melodies of an Atlantic
sea turtle

No regrets
home is heaven
carried with ease
and grace to anchor always
near the confluence of rivers
and trade winds

Feet firmly flat across
this no-man's land
the acrobat
with lockjaw and club foot
is surfing in the twilight   *without passport or apology*
                              in spiral flight

The skylark rides
the waves as always
resisting the force
feeding

The empire
in-breeding and the vulgar
'Lawd what a Saturday
night' feeling to reside above
the borders the boundaries
and the ball and chain

Breath bold folding over
the carpet goat-skin
the rocking chair of sorrel
petals shaped for comfort
in the dry season *here songs are sealed to furnish*
every room

The other stories
must be told

Always once upon
a time a journey

To where the urge
within must feed

And memory is made
from a web of razor grass

When speaking in whispers
or whistling the mystery of salt

And in corridors where
snow-filled tears have sat
entombed in paraffin fumes

There is always in the ebb
and flow

There is always a slant
a style a swing

Time tall eternal outstretched
the impossible is conquered
calling healing
calling healing
in the eye of the creator *here the welcome*
mat in place
takes a chorus
to the bridge

Today is Special

Today is special
without knowing

                questions follow
                the footsteps of saints
                the laughter of idiots
                the tears of the blessed

Today is special
without warning

                your words make
                a gentle wave
                calling like a beacon
                to water for parched lips

Today is special
without ceremony

                your presence
                finds new space
                nestled beneath the hardness
                in a shady place forgotten

Today is special
without fetter

                the seeker dances
                in the stillness
                that perfumed heart
                where every day resides

Dr Livingstone's Casebook

Housing Problems

Watch carefully where
you place the weight

Dreams have a way
of performing a balancing
sometimes they will tip toe
to the edge of the sheltering   standing
between cheap life
and its cold remembrance

Watch carefully as your
steps move to seal
the slippage in between
the worn-out grass   hardened
by its own promise
against the elements

Watch carefully as you
seek to find the escape
route to the unwelcomed
gateway in the roofing   where
it was thought nothing
could come in-side-ways   or any other way

Watch carefully as you
move along the ribs

They must be surgically touched
to give the assurance needed
nothing major here
a small stitching   there
a resetting into place
makuti fibres tested   by tremors and deceit

Watch carefully where
you place the weight

The artist raised a canopy
with subtle strokes
humour and sweat somehow
the harsh questions have come
to make patchwork
seem the only thing to do now

With tomorrow's rain
in the distance

This roofing above   the housing
with its cracking   and creaking
with the weight of dreams
perched like a bird   or a rock descending……

Watch carefully
Watch carefully where
you watch…….

Robbery

what will become   she said
of us under the strain

tearing at my voice   and the other voices
chorused in silence
all around

the slow decay
has long set in
like a habit sealed
in a paralysed limb

what will become   a hollow echo
said of us as another

art treasure is ripped   a thin veil of laughter
away and dumped
with its history

Retaking Buchanan

for Lindsay Barrett

there is double speak inside
these reports the punctuation
clinical and concealed beneath
deep foam and noise

Buchanan at 11am
on Sunday 4th April 1993
is official and waiting
for more orders

and as you know
another offensive is only
another terror trail
for the innocent

today Liberia
is a rebounding sermon

an enigma on the morning after
waiting for the architects

the breeze blocks
that are scattered here
among the sneering
skulls and children's toys
are questions lodged
like shrapnel in a crimson dawn

what difference does
it make a captain's log
a general's memoirs
another dispatch
from the front

the dinner guests
before the table spread
carry trophies of Biafra
and Katanga and more
among their treasures

by the sweat of their brow

                they eat

cultured in

                bigotry and ignorance

cultured in

                americo arrogance

cultured in

                missionary providence

by the sweat of their brow

                they eat flesh

and so it is
this scattering
when every now and then
the season of war
blowing hot
blowing cold

you keep your words
rooted as the flame
inside your chest
restlessly you move
in defiance of Berlin 1884
echoing…

                is who dem a tark to…
                you might say
                dem kiarn license
                mi mout
                dem kiarn license
                mi foot

salt water has never
dried upon your skin I say...

maybe someday
at evening light
when the sound of the market
place has been cleared away

maybe someday
at low tide when the mangrove
roots are bare and the oysters
ripe for picking

we will sit together
and chart the course within
where memory and music
made its first awakening

Buchanan on this Sunday
is official… is waiting…

Tears and Laughter Embrace in the Blood-Stained Forest

for Abdullah Ibrahim

the bloody dust
shifts in the wind
melody siren lifting
crashing across the tin
shack skyline
where Biko's foot
steps trace
ancestral pathways

even when necks
are tender
and stretched
like tendons
in a distant voice
the songs rebound
from the island stone

these are songs
that give children
peaceful nights
rock them to sleep
causing fear to flee
making room for people
to sit down
in solitude
and just touch
and just screeeeeaaaam!

bush man arrive
with news
gold miner
child father
night and day
worker arrive
with news

shit cleaner
baby minder arrive
with news
lonely wife
from alien homeland
dribbling children arrive
with news
grandmothers and grandfathers
storytellers and stone throwers
arrive with news

we
    have
        counted
many
     dead
we
    have
        counted
many
     dead

we have met
in Sharpeville
in Soweto
in Langa

Crossroads

in the belly of the earth
in the haunting church bell
cursing the air

we
    have
        counted
many
     dead
we
    have
        counted
many
     dead

another one
bites the dust

victim of alcohol
victim of gunshot
victim of diligent hangman

another one
bites the dust

victim of market prices
victim of apartheid stability
victim of buoyant credit card
victim of cash register overflow

we
    have
        counted
many
     dead

we
    have
        counted
many
    dead

charted many
bloodstained mountain
tracks to liberty
an African sketchbook
in the wind
life flutters
in the stillness
life flickers
in a sea
of fang tooth hypocrisy

we
    have
        counted
many
    dead
we
    have
        counted
many
    dead

assegai fingers pull
over ripe words
from ivory tongues
exploding like crystal
rain in the spine
the voice is hot
breath of township

cooking
        cursing
praying
        marching
defying
        bulldozer politics

the melody rushing
cool quiet silence
loaded with seeds
of wide awake morning
fanning a bush fire
telegraph untamed

and the way
I dance
and the way
I move
in the music
rhythm flow
so far away
defies the barriers
of sand
of propaganda
of sick minds

a slender light
a train whistle
speaks to me
in a breath of bloody
sweat and the spirit
song goes on

ah wanto kwela
wid you
ah wanto kwela
wid you
ah wanto kwela
wid you
ah wanto kwela
wid you… aaaah
ah wanto kwela
wid you
ah wanto kwela
wid you…
ah wanto kwela
wid you…

and the mountain
before us tonight
is spread out majestic
to cleanse the putrid legacy

the mountain before us
spreads out its blessing
a blanket across the acid wine fields
cooling your crusty fingertips

it is springtime
where the oceans meet
facing the window of the sacred tombs

Paper Clips are Precious in Rwanda

'Nothing can prepare one for the experience of genocide and the murderous campaign to eliminate political opposition in Rwanda. There are no words that can do justice to the anguish of the survivors and the cruelty of the killers.'
Death, Despair and Defiance –
Africa Rights Report, Rakiya Omar, 1994

how do you keep
things together
when the soul
is already ripped apart

rain
we welcome rain
on this fertile earth
we welcome rain

and the showers arrive
to take the smell
of bitter memories away

the eucalyptus is solemn
the banana leaves
are burdened with sorrow
human voices are raised
no further than a murmur
drowned out by the satellite
channels of world reports
nothing serious just sport

a smile
we welcome a smile
in the treacherous silence
we welcome a smile

but the wild west is everywhere
and 'this is Africa'
with slap-stick terror in the air

hugging to haunt
there is no escape
the deformed melodies
are abundant
as baptismal choirs sing
in pitiful whispers
with no relief from the demons
in occupation

light
we welcome light
into the heavy hearts
we welcome light

but in the dimness of dawn
the wounded soul is a dark
and hollow hole

a hall without mirrors
wedged between the lean
menus of dry bone soup
priced beyond the imagination
showers arrive to take
the smell and bitter
memories away
still the questions return

with the other eight
hundred thousand statistics
now heaped together
in an apologetic UN epitaph

there is a flatness
in the mountain landscape
nothing stands out
the heroes have not returned
from the nightmare

today we will try
to dream in volumes
rescued from the crimson night

today we will try
to shape the ragged syllables
into a landscape of sunflowers

tomorrow a patchwork
might reveal some beauty
a crescent light perhaps
a firmer footstep

how do you keep
things together
when the soul
is already ripped apart
paperclips are
precious in Rwanda
no sharp edges
just a cushion soft
to hold a hidden hand
somewhere outstretched
to fall and rest and guide
a smile

Tangled Melodies

I   Freetown Memories

It was as if
a bolt of lightning
had twisted itself
around the prophet
as he moved to the mountain
erasing faith
and strangling him
into submission
leaving the last note
of the proclaiming call
to prayer
hanging between
life and doom
mangled in the desert dust
leaving lorries
and the faithful stranded
with the burden of greed
abandoned to the pleasures
of dead conscience

Out of the morning
mist each day I watch
the orphans come
to consecrate their dreams

Like the wine of palm
promises flow sweet
then turn sour
by midday

On the verandas
lips are sweaty
with second-hand odours
and club sandwiches
spitting casually at the lepers
carting their paralysed
limbs they bow
to the claws of drought
like the broken
branch of a tree
or an antique
bronze of Benin
or a lamp post
hit by a drunken driver

At the desert's edge
Mercedes are stuck
in potholes
abandoned by all
except the unborn
who scrawl
"love is strange" across
the muddy windscreens

In the market place
old men gather
to count the heroes
of foreign wars
they sit among the flies
the casual glances
the indifferent stares
fermenting in the sun

The crowds gather
everyone comes
to hear tales
to live for a brief
moment to rest
in the shade

Lonely bush tracks criss
cross Harmattan voices
crack venting strange music
kicking up dust
in the pathway
of pompous motorcades
and polite conversation

Velvet appetites turn
sometimes disturbed
by the molten lava
flow of a river
with a bridge
that stops halfway
across their recreation

The backyard streets
spread untamed
and every face
conceals a minefield

II Child Servant, Child Slave, Child Soldier

At the age of ten
blindly charged with hate
he walks with the burden
of age in multiples
beyond his years

At the age of ten
she sits weary and without shade
clutching her womb
that has grown in multiples
beyond her years

The tears
that seal their hearts
are cold as rock
not knowing
the words of their knowing

There are no bed
time stories here
there is no once
upon a time
no call and response

The maternal choruses
have died somewhere
before the story began

Now the children
wear hand-me-downs
and the multiple
years of unburied corpses
carried as baggage
as trophies without glory

III Big Tree Party

Bought and sold
fig leaves are cheap
battle dress flimsy
but colourful in conceit

History built on
hand-me-downs ferment
and sags against
the weight of truth

we are having a party
a big tree party

Hear the cries of children
born spectators
at their own funeral

Hear the blind worshippers
scream their guilt
into leaking collection plates

we are having a party
a big tree party

The hills above
the horizon are no further
than a bag of rice away

But the harbour sharks
who speak with rotting
flesh between their teeth
stand guard with the stray dogs
the criminals and the crocodiles
ceremonial in their body odour

we are having a party
a big tree party

We fear the rain
and dread the sun
the taste of harvest
fruit sends a chill between
the tracks of memory
the odd legs
the misplaced hands
the scared faces

What litters the roadside
remains litter
in the cemetery of dreams
litter is everywhere

Tangled melodies
litter everywhere

In this after light we ask
for a straight path

In this after light we search
beyond the camouflage
for a simple needle and thread

In this after light
we must seek to breed
new joys and trust
the truth of touch

You cannot demand
a gift to give
is a blessing
is not a command

Juffure in the Tourist Season

at this time of year
Juffure is dusty
the mangoes are green
photo opportunities
are plentiful not far
a small stone throw away

across moody water
lies a derelict signpost
to civilisation
James Island the gate
way to a universe of choices
then and now

picture postcards
are gathered here
with forensic zeal

everyone wants
to contrive their own
piece of virgin truth

everyone wants
to call out
Kunta Kinteh's name

like phoney French
on hotel menus
at this time of year

Juffure is a muffled minaret
where dreams are bought and sold

Jane

Paradise she had been told
was not to be missed
Get there at any cost
the island is unspoilt
Green and innocent
her anxiety overwhelmed
And the small plane
touched down like a fly
On a cushion
nothing seemed out of place

The airport – wow!
let's see it all
It was a nearly straight
road small hills
And a few potholes
slowed the journey
As night fell suddenly
she felt cheated
And scrambled to catch
the fading noise of the town

A small distance
away from the lodge
The paved road sunk
into a mass of bush
Dirt tracks hedged
with malarial puddles
The stench of the fermenting
town limits gave way
To an impenetrable distance
beyond unspoilt and uninviting

Jane turned back
a smirk smeared across her face
All the way back
to the lodging room
Nothing much there she thought
the generator rumbled all night
As a dim reading lamp
made the night bearable
Mosquitoes make bad companions
with their selfish taste

Talkative at breakfast
tips on safe sex
Mix casually with memories
of dangerous diving elsewhere
Flight schedules are consulted
urgently there is a need
For some relief to feed
the creeping boredom
For an exit to somewhere more familiar
where the customer is always bloody right!

Arriving at Bagamoyo

Bagamoyo,
place of rest
if only for awhile

It is low tide
and the footprints
chart maps way beyond
the shore line
into the depths of despair
into the dungeons of memory and stories
ancient in their twists and turns and insides out

Bagamoyo,
place of rest
where the heart
beat slows down
to an anxious pulse

Dr. Livingstone, We Know

Dr. Livingstone you are mesmerised
                               we know
The legacy of confusion
                               the unpaid debt
Dr. Livingstone you are mesmerised
                               we know
The confusion remains
                               a heavy burden

a stroll at sunset
a little rooftop
romance after dark
on perfumed carpets
every step measured
in the currency of conquest

Karibu doctor
Karibu bitter medicine

                               we know

Like all good redeemers
With an eye for a good deal

                               the unpaid debt

Buy on bright days
Sell before the wind shifts

                               we know

The curse of noble lineage
That defined the species

                               a heavy burden

Conversations are careless
in their contempt
Laughter is as rude and chilling
as the snarl of a bull dog
Nothing is as it seems
except for the order of service

We know
the unpaid debt

We know
a heavy burden

Bagamoyo Smile

ndugu
you are smiling
and I wonder
if it is something about
me staring at you
across the centuries
with all the baggage civilized
complacency can bring

is this the costumed
drama of another age
fancy dressed up
to mock the contortions
of this modern life I do

not understand
this carnival the silent
snigger against the background
hip hop ragga music

did I hear
a question
probing the pleasure
of my global village dance

ndugu
you smile
the chains
are polished now
all jazzed up
as ornaments they mock
your rough metallic burden

to be captured here
as there what distance
lies between us
both how long
is a piece of chain
you smile again...
na wewe, jina lako nani?

The End of Slavery in Zanzibar

In Stone Town alleyways	noisy secrets and bells
ply their innocence	with a solemn air
here I now commemorate
a moment of regime change
that raised a white flag above
a rubble of contentment to proclaim	a history seeped in
	consecrated villainy

Commemorate this day	in short light hours
the Sultan is in retreat	without a cloak
or sweet perfume around his feet
a blazing trail came
with holy water knocking
as artillery crushed the trade	in cloves that fuelled
	the spice of island life

Time had come with naval crusade	seeking new stocks
new shares and the glory	of new denominations
it set about to reign and tame
to school the natives
into willingness bearing
their fate by imperial design	with banners unfurled
	in gunpowder smoke

The sultan said he was satisfied	as cool breeze from the sea
returned to calm	his complacency
as he slept at dusk a long
cathedral shadow cast
fresh light on the market-place
it lit the path for boy scout regiments	to plant Britannia's traces
	in another foreign field

The Sultan's Ruins

The sultan's ruins stand
precarious on the backs
of termites scavenging blindly
feasting on freedom
until they bloat and die
without ceremony or cry

> *It is bath-time again*
> *party planning*
> *body tanning*
>
> *The passion oils now float*
> *into the midday sun*
> *deaf to the ebb of low tide*

The sultan's ruins stand
cold and inviting
curious stares come to probe
the stagnant legacy of excess
sealed in footnotes
on the tombs of sinking graves

> *And even the fragrance*
> *of an enlightened soul*
> *may turn to stench and die*
>
> *If light and life*
> *finds no fertile breath*
> *within the sustainer's shade*

It is bathing time again
each season
overtakes another
the sun and moon
maintain their order
the Qiblah point is clear

Salme's Night Flight

She skipped the rooftops
lightly as a bird
across the surf

And when her slender
ankles secured her
safely a chill set in

servants can be bought
the grandeur of aristocratic
taste can cool
the sting of exile
only for awhile

The jasmine of her footprints
left a trail
so sweet the whispering
desire for return
still haunts the ocean winds

Death of a Neem Tree

So much promise   so much hope

All around the season
is abundant with rain
And the earth is full   fertile with expectation
and the harvest of faithfulness

Look at the eyes   they smile at each other

Carelessly sinking into shyness
innocently winking and closing
Seeing nothing
but the blessing to come

Now it is no more   whispered a bird shrieking
a song from a broken branch

Too dry to hold
the pain of casualness

The leaves have fallen too   without warning or newsflash
as if at daybreak

The sky had opened
into splinters instead of rain

A library is on fire
The healing hand is paralysed

So much promise   so much hope

Now only a desolate stump
green grass has sprung
from the roots
like a prosperous graveyard

No need for an axe   no need for a tomb

The all-in-one great tree
stands still anchored

Into the heart of the earth
like a lighthouse without a lamp

After the Rain

I

the figures do not add up
the sums are pear shaped
calculators and computers
buckle under

the imbalance
the weight keeps shifting
jumping and rolling
around sometimes

it is sexy
most times
it is dead

warm salaams tend
to evaporate in the heat
leaving a trail infected
by the language of dependency

a friend in deed
is as good as the sticking
plaster in hand

looking around town
trying to find a bargain
the shelves are packed
with razor blades

in air conditioned alleyways
vendors offer abundant
advice on shaving
in the dark

II

'*What is life,*
Life is a dream'
Black Uhuru

the dawn chorus
at alfajiri hails me
from my restless sleep
the call promises
with patience
with steadfastness
success in faith

along the way
the day beckons
and this life presents
itself in all that is seen

a ragged cart man
drags his burden
of second-hand goods
his life like local music
is officially worth
no more than a one night
hotel room in low season

III

she walks with grace
and as if in prayer
frankincense and myrrh
are wrapped around her body
with the care of pure music

like an oasis
the jasmine petals
at her feet are cooling
in the midday heat

I wish to hear
her heart's exquisite voice

If only the market
noise was not so loud

Starehe – Nafsi Poa

boB mArley sang
in his head
and said
doWn here
in jaH Mek Yah
doWn here
in da ghee Toh
we sufFa
we suffA
we dey soH faaAr

in his head
he said
dis is Afrika
not knowing the full
swelling of the word
sound that was causing
him to hop
and drop walking
in the same rough
road where only
a reggae bAss
bounce could get
you oVah and unto
the flat and level
without tilting you under
the edge of the world

Dat is how jaH
Mek Yah come to
be in Afrika
and not anywhere
that Columbus
settle and set
in a tomb
and so it was
inA power failing
hE discovered that
a spark in di wiring
was lighter than hiM

The Border

straight lines drawn
across a blank page
the colonial rulers
callous calculating and clinical
with their rules in hand
sword scalpel and howitzer

they measured the balls
of the natives
calibrated the temperature
of their shit
and in the earth
dug graves for the supplicants

today the squeak and squelch of designer
shoes track across the soggy Rwanda earth
to Congo alleyways and back again
between corpses and compass points
we will find King Leopold
a Stanley Living
stone Cameron Burton all
Wisemen of the apocalypse

all Rhodes lead to the high table
spread with flags of surrender
ceremonies colourful in the filth
of triumphant clapping hands

they retrace the lines
and the lies
with reverence
with obedience
with cross-eyed squint
self-recognition is sideways

indecent as the glare
of a lynch mob
Africa hangs suited
and tied swaying in submission
without peace
dumbfounded by the juju of maps

Digging
Down

Taking the Medicine

for Shake Keane

There have been many reported
sightings of this man

with distinct features
definitely Antillean
slightly mid-Atlantic
definitely African

                                      no doubt
                                      in transit

who sings in his sleep
walking his tone is warm
and known to regularly
break ice

There have been many reported
sightings of this man

at high tide he
sits like a rock
above the squall

at low tide
his footprints remain
like crab tracks
circling in all

                                      directions

unravelling the past

                                      and futures
                                      of today

weblike the riddles roll
off the feathered plumes
of colonial monuments
into the trade winds

There are many reports
about reported
sightings of this man

long pants too short
shoes that fit too big
shirt stiff with cassava starch

the boy was over
eating since before

                                        birth no doubt
                                        forced ripe

he took everyone by surprise
and whistled without
moving his lips

                                        well

There are many reports
about reports
in strange handwriting

government officials
and civil servants
labour to account for the leakage
the presence is everywhere

in every wooop
in every waarp
in every doo-daa-doo

he still sings
in his sleep

                              walking

he still whistles
without moving his lips

                              water

he said
with no visible
sign of thirst

                              water

how could you
imagine life
without drinking
from a volcanic

                              spring

The Journey

for S.B.

it was like getting back
clear eye vision again
after digging out the gravel

and when the weather cleared
and calm returned
to bring cool breeze
the hardest thing
was not knowing
the sight of flowers growing

it was as if sleep
could steal reality
from right under/over you
leaving only a frail
faith in the gap
between night and next day
where the memories lay
like eggs in a tenement yard
rocking to a weekend sigh
over an evening meal
cooked all day with love

> *here soh*
> *we mek do*
> *wid likkle*
> *an' sometime*
> *not much*

it was here you met
the spider spirit
the boat and cart builder
the washerwoman vendor

the time was concrete
and the river stone
smooth from beating
it was not a dream

the time was blue light
flashing gunshot trailing
gunman dog chasing
man chasing phantom

in the crossfire
it was money or life
but in your pockets
only bread crumbs

hard dough
like everywhere else
water was scarce
regular blackouts
confounded nature
the trickle down
locked in a constant battle
with the blocked sewer

your journey knew
no bounds to spiral flight

still there was a need
for a homecoming
there was a passion
to reorder the mumbo jumbo
embalmed in camphor

as evening grew
with the coming time
of parting your footsteps
led to a marble pavement
overlooking the river
the rancid water barely
managed a ripple across
its breath stretched a shadow
a tower of high culture stood
anticipating a storm

in the silence
there was nothing
to pursue or reclaim
only a brief handshake
will mark the place
where your breath

sank in
to the fountain

Dreamworker

for Martin Carter

His suit is cut
with immaculate style
elegance is stitched in
to the seams.

The khaki is like his face
durable and not what it seems
so the greetings come
with songs of hope
with choruses sealed
in firm handshakes
that slap and caress
like the inherited
land of rivers and rock.

And so to sleep
is to dream of builders
more skillful
than a hurricane tail wind.

And so to sleep
is to dream of Kaieteur's
grandeur as a measure
for the soul's aspirant flight.

Kaieteur Callaloo

for Aubrey Williams

In passing: a brief embrace
                    warm like creek
                    water ripples rolling
                    to the melody of bird
                    song in flight

In an effort
to retrace swollen footsteps
I stood still
with loaded breath

                the sound of water
                everywhere inching
                eating away at instincts
                so sharp they nestle
                on the solitary
                hinges of floodgates

Kaieteur's seething cauldron
chills the noontime rest

In the hour-glass
the rising tide hints: a rapturous whirlwind

                between breaking
                                  cane
                between breaking
                                  rock
                between broken

                                  clay pot

Between now and coming time

                                  rapids rejoice

Small Island Pride

there is a storm
lurking on the ocean
restless winds
have come
as a warning

last night loose
tongues damaged
something funny
no one knew
what had hit

                    where
                    there

is a storm
lurking in the waves
washed up in between
rum punch and bar-b-q
on the sun-kissed sand
a rusty church bell
leaves a blood-stained echo
in every ebb and flow

                    here
                    there

is a storm
lurking in the voices
deserted by language
tongue tip is
                duty free

no responsibility
              sold
and spread out
              like cow

skin in the sun
stiff with vexation
but obedient to the narcotic
hand of dollar exchange

        here
        there

a storm lurks
behind a silent conspiracy

        the island
        they say

is a showpiece for democracy
a free country

the rich eat plenty
the poor hope for a decent funeral

until then they wear
their pride like sunday
best taffeta

        yes lawd
        ah wish di damn
        precha woulden taark
        so lang
        mek mi belly
        bawl wid gas

a storm lurks
un
   seen
un
   heard

Approaching the Savannah from the Middle Passage

the night seems sleepless
now the nebular sky charts
languages to be translated
in ethereal moments
beyond temporal scales

in the chilly air
melody is quilted with whispers
wild like brush
strokes of a fugitive dawn

this ecstatic laugh and cry
this unfinished ending restlessly
compels frayed nerve-ends
against known limits of ease

                    every breath
                    a fluttering footstep
                    into future light

                    every sigh
                    a bead of sweat
                    into memory's ocean

where dreams
and death
lose their sequined
shadows and are reborn
as clarion doves

Tongues: Drum Sounds and Firewood

it is a hundred
degrees in the shade
the temperature is persisting
out of season
the island earth
hungers with uncertainty

waiting for a breeze
waiting for a downpour

talking in tongues
comes naturally

ole bakra
still walks around
with sweaty exercise book
scribbling with spit
on pencil point
his eyes darting
about the steamy market yard
not much has changed

the balance sheet
the fork-tongue
the fish bone
in the throat

half Nelson
half Columbus
half Pirate
half Mongrel

they roam the streets
and the airwaves

in the after smoke I walk
listening to hearts
and the cane-trash
faces of history

in the after smoke I walk
talking in tongues comes naturally

Pasero

all that separated
him from the grimy streets
outside was a dirty
window glass

no one saw his face
the fire and blood
surging from his navel
to sustain sanity

                    yet strangers usually
                    asked questions

                    are you
                    from Timbuktu

without a sense of knowing
that the name
was real and he
would want to say

                    yes but
                    usually shrugged
                    his shoulders
                    to avoid forensic surgery

survival is a game of protecting
pearls from swine

now he walks with measured
rhythm between places
felt hat tipped
slightly to one side

        alert and knowing
        the solid texture

        tempered by a long
        journey of exile

        his leather shoes built
        to outlive human frailty

        his suit hangs as it
        would on a younger man

a brittle frame wrapped
in tailored elegance now
possessing a breast pocket
loaded with a gold watch
ticking away to the next
stop beyond the grave

Heritage

your hands
have built cities
fought wars
served forgivingly
to the enemy
turned stones
moulded bread

now in the heat
of time longer
than rope
the bond
is fever tense
in balance
and flight I

clench my fist
it sings

the melody
is your gift

Abstract

for Joe Harriott

I

di island
mountain side
an' gully bottom
have it own
blue an' red
even sometimes white
green misty morning

see it
from a distant angle
it doan have
meaning or sign
unless you touch
di whole
ah it mento swing
shaped in di root
seed jam down
pon bare side wall

di john crow
get confuse
when more food
dedeh than
him belly full
so dis one step
three four blues
is a bright eye tune
for a secret lover

hear me now
hear me now

nani bird in flight
nani bird in flight

oya oya
oyaoooh!
oh
   yeah!

II

wanted to
write you
a song
melody and rhythm
laced in your plaited
knots of hair
sensuous as lips
touching surf spray

wanted to
write you a song
wanted to
see you dance
a soft rapid
river flow
sensuous as lips
touching surf spray

wanted to
write you
a song
to see you
dance and break
the silence
lodging in between
the rise and falling
away promise of sensuous
lips touching surf spray

silence
                    each night
passes into
                    silence
each night
                    passes

the daydreams stagger
to meet the glaring
crowds like sour
milk on welcome mats
and good intentions
are a crime

Monk's Mood

how could this man
come in here staggering

>	dancing and twisting
>	shouting between
>	whispers of foot-fall

how could he
come in here

>	and dare
>	to turn the stein
>	way back to front

don't give a damn
then leave
then leave
a note sitting

>	not just one
>	but a colossal
>	wrap of percussive melody

all in one

>	some marimba
>	scribbles without
>	saying a word

except don't
read newspapers
unless you find them
discarded in the street

Eyes

for Lester Bowie

there are many names
for the face of that sound

depends on how the pepper
seasons your throat
how the gumbo heats your blood
how the greens and rice
drum roll their way up front
next to steaming fish
full of reasoning

then again it might be
the long sea journey
and the not-accustomed-to-land-so-strange
and the getting used to it
with foot cramp
and a choir of tongues
so sweet but searching
for a mean chord

and all this while
everyone was gathered as a witness
and the executioner was condemned
and the face of the sound
rung bells from belly deep

a shower more dread
than a thousand galaxies erupted
a mystery perhaps
aging and resurrecting
the word a golden
thread of clay
a seed of breath singing
beneath the pestle of time

Travelling Miles With You

a Conversation with Miles and Cassandra

the doooooo
WHAP sings
it stings
the scars
between the COLD sweat
nothing is wasted
no thing is wasted

it fills
the EMPTY spaces
with simplicity
soft as a cat's
paw it struts
a serious STUFF
the doooooo whap sings

IT is precise
as starched
and pleated shirts
holding the RAGE
balancing
on the be
of the bop

you have SPOKEN of rivers
you have spoken of the night
turned inside OUT

this long blue
NOTE the trace
in BLOOD you see
is it a foetus screeeeeming
to be born
or a corpse laid out
on an altar erupting

the dooooo WHAP sings
it stings the scars
it sings for the rail
road to freedom

walking this tight
rope holding
my breath
our eyes
meet we ask
each other
the way ahead

you have
spoken of rivers
YOU have spoken of the night
and now

if you SWING
in the breeze
like a BIRD
on a branch
feel the earth
and the flowers
smile for MILES

let me greet
you where peace
rains in the desert
beneath the crescent shade
the calligraphy of clouds
join the sea and sky
tonight destiny visits

Desert Flower

She is a desert flower
tired and lonely
in her joy and terror
She is a mermaid washed
up between the congestion
of four wheel traffic

behind her eyes
hollow buildings crumble
every second on the down
beat foundations float
in the whirlwind
that guides her journey
retracing the paper trail
of ancestral dreams

In the city
she finds peace
at the junction of uncertainty
Familiar faces are magnified
into fragments of a future
past that shouts a solemn smile

She is a desert flower
    she is a mermaid
Dancing it seems
    frozen in flight

her footsteps will leave
no memory except
the nameless jagged smear
dragging itself into oblivion
she will send no postcards
emails will return
asking for certainty
that no faith can provide

For her the time of day
will come and go
Weather forecasts will make no
difference though a chill turns heads

Flashing wild signals
as recognition is betrayed
In a casual wink beneath
the fault line of despair

She is a desert flower
    she is a mermaid
Dancing it seems
    frozen in flight

The Rose

Watching you
glow shyly
opening and inviting
light between the shadows

You spiral out
and burst causing
jewels to smile
in my heart

Boomerang

for Pitika Ntuli

getting your self
into trouble again
is a nice statement
for breaking ice

a kind of greeting
before introducing
electric shock into
an accusing body

this limited but flexible
vocabulary has been touted much
from moral high ground
and ventilated interrogation rooms

used as a democratic
exercise a laxative
fine tuned on the road
from Cairo to the Cape

> yah mi bro
> your accent is an accentuation
> tempered forged and recycled
> florescent with every echoing scream

getting your self
into trouble again
is a nice statement
for breaking ice

a greeting

> tempered
> forged
> recycled

a chilling invitation to dance

Send me a Bouquet of Bones

'Only when you drink from the river of silence shall you indeed sing.'
Kahlil Gibran

Strong tides disguised
within calm seas
Sails flapping
thunderous and blind
As heavy currents
pull us under

The chilly winds
come and go leaving
A knife edge
lingering like lightning
In search
of fatal release

The chilly winds play
tricks with laughter and tears
Sails flapping around
fragile in peacefulness
As compass points change
course without warning

It will be night again
before ease arrives
With low tide creeping
there will be many seasons
Before the moon
escapes its shadow

If nothing is left
    after the scavengers have gone

Send me a bouquet of bones
    that sing the music of flutes

Interludes

Requiem for the Widow or a Colonial Jumbie

'They have made the degradation and humiliation of their daily lives their own tourist attraction.'
Jamaica Kincaid

>the sun sets with painfully long
>shadows drawing mouldy footnotes
>from the scattered island shores
>
>comings and goings
>meet a nameless past
>in a nameless present

once an industrious concubine
these days
she spends her time

baking cakes
baking tarts

little things

that used
to make sense

at tea parties

she bakes cakes
she bakes tarts
no one will eat

now

she does elementary
arithmetic instead of saying
grace before meals

in the midday shade
a tourist passes by staring
enquiringly the widow
answers genuflecting

history is my
blunt cutlass

she speaks of suicide
she speaks of murder
she speaks of bouncing

                  her toe
                  on a big stone

do you know
she asks the tourist
the name of this place

                  it is an island
                  a wandering sea urchin

came upon it one day
in fourteen ninety-three

he stepped ashore
named it in the name of himself
the queen he served
and the god who served her

clinical massacres telegraphed
the native peoples
into a crimson twilight

country above self
liberty or death

a fountain of salt
gushed inward from the earth
raising monuments in stone
sacraments of blood

the widow welcomes
her supplicant visitor

the lord's prayer
is on the tip
of her tongue

her daily bread
her cup that once runneth
over in torrents

the remembrance clings
like a pertinent sentry
keeping out local distractions

for security she has a dish
full of the world

endless channels
of modern life

she finds comfort
in melodramas of neurosis
in circus parades of evangelist

her old house stands
listless with the burden

in the afternoon shade
a steelband passes by
without stopping
the widow laments

she has few possessions left
the boy who cuts the grass
went yesterday
to the beach

                he watches bath towels
                he cleans the sand
                he likes being near the water
                he wants to live in America

she does not remember
his name
she does not know
his name

she calls him
              John!

a madman answers
one foot in the gutter
one foot dragging behind
the steelband rush

the widow asks
how many times
have I run a pencil through
his hair before morning prayer

the tourist is astonished
the widow turns sour

steelband music
infectious laughter
washes over her

                like a hurricane flood
                people relieve themselves
                in front of her door

she blames them
for the rotting wood
that is her home

the tourist smiles
picturing herself
on the sun-kissed beach

she pictures herself
crossing a boulevard
walking briskly worried
about her savings
and the cost of turkey
for thanksgiving

the widow turns sour again
this time with envy

she beckons the tourist pass
treacherous floorboards pointing

look at one of my past students
a promising choirboy now turned
stupid by an addiction to begging
and speaking in disembodied syllables

he says
the island is his own

he recognises only those things
ordained in the name of himself
the queen he serves
and the god who serves her

the cemetery buries
itself in disgust

one night the national
library lit the sky in flames
no fire has burned
with such brilliance

on this island
ancestral lives are now silent smoke
paradise is peacefully festering
like an amputated limb misplaced
in the heat of a hasty retreat

what's left is a trinket
a flag a colourful
but flimsy fig leaf
a sugar and water bonus

the widow is sweating cold
as shadows lengthen she fears
the language of the night
especially when it rains vex… vex… vex

the tourist trembles
she was told of adventure

          rain forest
          wild monkeys
          endless pleasures
          tax free

the widow smiles knowingly
for the first time
in her usual way
she sighs as if to say

this is a small place
this is a fowl coop
in somebody's backyard

it takes a hurricane
to make this place famous
it will take a massacre
to stamp the name upon a map

the tourist watches
uneasy and sweaty

there are children
passing the veranda
their school uniforms
have worn out their stiffness
dust gathers in open sores
they look familiar

these passing children
are giggling into a void

they will grow up
with short memories
subtle hips and an appetite
for plane tickets

as the tourist leaves
another panel falls free
from the veranda lattice work

the widow is not
smiling she stops
to remove a dead wasp
from the plastic flowers

she bids her kindred
soul goodbye

send a postcard she says
and the latest
price of insecticide

she whispers a prayer
in the name of herself
the queen she serves
and the god who serves her

In the Story So Far

'Poetry arrived in search of me…'
Pablo Neruda

I

standing at the crossroads
the hour of choice chimes
across deserted doorways sand
storms through gaping windows

the signposts have been used
to sell counterfeit identities
the hurricane lamp light
is now the nightshade for whores

>   here I pause
>   wishing to recall
>   wishing to retrace footsteps
>
>   to unlearn
>   to recognise
>   to gaze

without blinking rudely
when light is scarce

II
in the story so far
mother of my days
she carries a water pot

the journey never
strained her smile

while others complained
of battle fatigue

    cracked lips
    skin scaling
    from fingers she said

her soul danced
in the window of the full moon sky

    her body
    oil-lit the night

and at dawn she distilled
her kisses in embryos of dew

    here I pause
    wishing to recall
    wishing to retrace

footsteps at the first
cutlass swing descending
upon broken syllables

    clinging
    to cane
    root

looking up from the muted
leaves beneath my feet
rain clouds gather above
the mountain tops parched and dry

the air is feather
light a flood threatens
to wash the weak
and feeble out to sea
sharks and rotten timber
await their coming

at the crossroads
a funeral passes
the grave is at my feet
between my toes

the earth is moist
the earth is ash
the earth is lifeless clay

it sticks to my skin
it congeals my blood

the funeral passes
away into confused sermons
leaving a drizzle
in the misty air

III

    in the story so far
    she carries a water pot
    holding the ocean
    and its fuming currents

her breath touched my lips
where dry blood had left a shell

silence shed its muted sound
like skin drums in flight

through steamy forest nights
and something thundered

    roaring deep
    journeying to somewhere

the path before me loomed familiar
the path before me stood calm with mystery

a stillness between
departure and arrival

a bridge of corpses
balancing between
my delicate strides

IV

what meaning makes these tongues persist
what power tries to force a sound
to stamp a shadow here

what volcanic passion seeks melodious release
what ecstatic faith commands
vision in/to action

in the soul
the healer's hand
moulds fire
like bread for food

> in the story so far
> the old woman
> closed her eyes
> raised her head
> gave her breath
> back to the eternity

the wind made music
sometimes calm
sometimes gentle
sometimes with the fury of an awakening
re-arranging the unbalanced ocean tide

against the silhouette of her face
my fingertips took flight

> her body
> oil-lit the night
> engulfing me
> in an embryo of dew

> her own pain and praise
> sealed with a nimble
> knife and fever
> thirst within my spine

From a Long Line of Soldiers

for a man called Blues

From a long line of soldiers
you have come
and now dear brother
you will enter the silent chamber

With bare chest
shouting your name
With clenched fists
strumming a road-march
With a stick-fighter's footsteps
that have scorched
a path with flambeau giant
light against the night

Into the silent chamber
you will go on the tail
wind of a hurricane

You will go with damp
earth wrapped
around your feet

Leaving the smell of volcanic
sulphur in the air
a j'ouvert mask at the roadside
proclaims past victories
that have conquered all
except the self

Somewhere in the wild echoes
your slippery footsteps
will be retraced
through the secret tracks and alleyways
that criss-cross the quilted signature
you have left behind

From the precipice of incomprehension
the names of things that have been jumbled
the labels turned inside out and crumpled
will have to be seduced into speech
from the pain of your broken guitar strings
From the precipice of incomprehension
I search the memory left in your wake
the laughter and the trembling handshake
gripping for as long as able to remind
or to seize a rare moment of truth

I search the quilted signature
You have left behind

Like someone touched
by a spirit or a thunderbolt
a lunatic shouts hearing
the solitude of your silence
and the chorus responds
as if compelled…

Together we sit barefooted
swinging just above the water's edge
and the sea with one eye squinting
beats against the rock
with knowing assurance
The ebb and flow reveals
the stains of today's sacrifice
primordial and permanent
in their innocence

From a long line of soldiers
You have come dear brother

and now…
the silent chamber…
the melody of your pain…

There is a kite in flight
with loose threads dancing
in flames against the sun

Inside the solitude of your silence
I hear swift and agile footsteps
A laughter that chases
Shadows from the night

Inside the solitude of your silence
The weight of burdened years is balanced
Against the memory of a fresh breeze
Warmed by a melodic note of your music

A rare moment of truth
royal as the coconut palm
in the calm of the after peace

One Season of Voyages

Departure-Distance-Destination

in this remembrance
there comes an invitation
it comes as legends do
with persistent footfall
splintering the certainty
encased in fragile limbo years

I return the gratitude walking
upright into the astonished crowd
I return as witness
straddling the ocean void

I return as stone
skipping across wind currents
I return as moonlight
skating settled sand dunes

in this remembrance
the head that wears tinsel
and exile is a twilight star
among the naked and the leftovers
it is an irritant pleasure found
scratching in the empire dust

in this remembrance
there are destinies designed
and monuments built
about legends told in rock
that stood against the corroding
imperial march across time

I return as moment
sinking taproot
into mineral core
I return as student
mindful of conformity
that deforms
I return as native dancer
more acrobatic than mummified
straight jacket

Nationals-Returning Residents-Aliens

the bags and baggage
hand luggage and gifts
are not always in the same
place things and thoughts get
re-routed with wrong labels
in the wrong hands sometimes
not handled with care or twisted
into new shapes on inspection

sniffer dogs tracking
the Atlantic undercurrent
and the monsoon wind of messages
sent ahead sometimes hears sounds
and echoes of their own invention
some arrivals they fear bring
the ocean's secrets set firm in coral
footprints to clog the cluttered carousel

a stranger recognizes my face
trying to break out I stretch
out my hand to make a mark
still flying to the shore surfing
into her simple story with much
more left unsaid now returning
she also must read right and wrong
while overweight and already late

more familiar edging forward
boxes must be ticked to record
time coming must be stamped
wide open the believer must
walk on water if necessity says
there needs to be a helping
hand a photograph or something
more to fill a void or confiscate

aliens schooled with short
pants and lotion handy tan
smile and hurry to the sun
it withers into wrinkled costumes
and options as real as mosquitoes
returning to revisit broken black
boards and the fish gut
opportunity for the economy

The Marketplace

welcome to the marketplace
where fear and favour mingle
with aid and treachery
bad bulls and wild sheep hang
upside down sneering
at forced stomach removal

the billboards new and erect
parade their changing colours
from safari cool to post-colonial
khaki drill development roaming
with impunity stitched up into
sweaty friendship dollar bills

second-hand clothes
do not fit me well
I do not get the thrill
there is only the shiver
that death on a road can bring
with good fortune for hyenas

these roads I learn were built
for fast moving motorcades
and presidents rushing away
from the governed mass
their caterpillar tracks leave no magic
carpet between the mattress and the mat

when night comes I hear signs
left by the butcher's knife
a soft voice saying nothing salutes
with both hands and rattling coins
that hold no maps or lamplight smoke
to place a stepping stone or call collect

it is peaceful here   yet so many expectant faces
and the mud splashing march
past of investors licensed to rob

it is peaceful here   yet so much push and pull
until a stare becomes a stand
to anchor firm against migrating wealth

it is peaceful here   with urgency jostling
in the shadow play behind
the high street hollow-gram

it is peaceful here   with anxiety juggling
until I asked
about the air conditioning

The Will to Walk

the mirrors scattered like abandoned beads
casts shadows against the sun and river roar
clear light across my face
at every roadblock
the hired rifleman
arrives barefooted and bold
in his benefactor's service

there is no porter column or caravan train
no branded beast with imperial flag unfurled
just clear light across my face
the sentry did not agree
in his book and matching
fingerprints a mark of metropolitan
exhaustion brings taxation

the well-trained man in charge has no time for prisoners
like rattlesnake in uniform he is self-assured
this is no lounge for transit
it is a bridge from which choice
will hang and dangle with a promise
or sit sucking salt at sunset
in the time-zone of no man's land

among the evening debris the beguiled and the snared
the bemused traders and the left behind
clear light and my face
with nothing to declare
except a state of emergency
the cost of a warm beer foams
flat against my will to walk

Zawadi Ya Zenj/A Gift of Zanzibar

for Maalim Idris

The alleyways in Stone Town
weave messages from afar
opening solid Swahili doors
to well-worn floors where knowledge
at the feet of sheikhs spreads widely
and speaks across the quilted roof tops

Every gift is a new breath
a small exchange of light
given in a whisper it arrives
like a fable folded with violins clashing
into resplendent khanga colours
and soaring voices in a monsoon breeze

From outstretched hands the gift is offered
without ceremony or excessive speech

The music fills the spaces where treasures
cling to cobwebs in high beamed homes

How strange the libraries
reside in silent corners
huddling there and condemned
to the shade like a wishing-well
with pasted posters peeling
and polite platitudes for the day-tripper

Ferry Crossing

In a hurry
    to beat the setting sun

Against the wind
    the captain signs a pact

With voices steeped
    in secrets of a thousand nights

The cargo surrenders
    and heads bow heavy

In plastic bags
    for nursing comfort

An ocean rises
    to write its music

Skipping octaves high
    and low semi-tones unbending

Odd knees buckle
    to resist the rending

Sad and sullen
    are the songs arriving

In the stories and tears
    worn deep into travelling faces

Askari

Askari   what do you see far off
              what demons have returned from wondering

Askari   what do you see near
               in the city's concrete cluttering

You are ice monument
in the sun frozen
in time without name
like turtle shell endangered
you are poised at peace
knee bent at the altering

Askari   king's African or native
               son of Empire procured

Askari   uniform tooth chipped
              a time and youth clipped

At the round-about
road where traffic fumes
in memory's sinking sand
return resides in the fallow
anthem of a pauper's pension
plan with elastic strings attached

Home is the final
station where trenches
and impotent regulation rifle
have come to rest in tin cup
tenements sky scraping one
phantom tower after another

Arusha

At the foothills of Kili Kibo peak
among the verdant valley ways
low cloud and a challenging chill reside

Ancient wisdom I am told
moves in concentric circles
with intent like memory in the blood

There was a time when hands horizoned
in all directions and the summit was aflame
A future found the cradle rocks
billowing at Butiama and beyond

It looped across the savannahs
meeting the coastal ebb and flow
Where buibui draped women who know
raised uncompromising battle banners

Foreign flags sailed away one
night as the winds changed course
A new story found its seeds
in a language reclaimed to serve

Arusha fathomed a fountain-head for destiny
where valley ways converged
It bridged the borders and the mountain
spoke with deep crystal dignity

With low cloud hanging hazy against
the clamour a restless hoe struck a rock
Where promise should reside the city clock
is now blind in corporate window dressing

In Arusha conferences and convocations
come and go seasonal and searching
Across the withering years
long shadows wait for the prodigal

Treasures

clutching a solid leather bag tight
skin holding a message bottled
and bobbed it braved the ocean tide
to settle in the sinuses of well-worn African hide

the tree stump here
the balancing rock face there

These simple things
remind me of you…

the sacred earth carried beyond
lessons learnt by perfect rote
concealing names fashioned for eternity
signpost the precipice and gateway signals

a taste of pepper near
a sharp tongue without fear

These simple things
remind me of you…

in the legends built on adventure tales
dungeons are erected with angular steel
in Berlin's bargain basement
the spoils were managed with historic
zeal they laid their tracks to criss-cross severed heads upon a stake
and a tailwind of fever and disease

trans-migrations now as in the loaded
traveller's log seek refuge in diplomacy
where land was claimed a place
is fenced a tent is pitched securely
pegged to the ground with native frame the relic certainty in decay weighs
heavy along its mythic snailing way

in my treasures carried for the journey
bitter cassava and black aloes preserve
integrity and the star-gazer's curiosity
in things forbidden by clergy and laity

the self-serving tyrannies
the soul-selling missionaries

These simple things
remind me of you...

Notes

Marcus Garvey Stood on Basseterre Bay Road reflects on an online reprint of a report about Garvey's visit to Basseterre, St. Kitts published in *The Union Messenger* of 3 November 1937 and reprinted in the Mutual Improvement Society magazine January 1993.

Minister Farrakhan and the Steelband is a comment on the experience of making a return 'home' visit, inspired by Louis Farrakhan's visit to St. Kitts & Nevis, the birthplace of his mother, in December 2011.

Wild Fires at the End of Summer was written in the wake of the 'riots' that flared in London and other British cities during August 2011 following the shooting of a black man by police in Tottenham.

Retaking Buchanan contemplates a news report about Buchanan, a city in Liberia where a major battle in that country's civil war was fought in 1993.

Paper Clips are Precious in Rwanda was written after a short stay in Rwanda, November/December 1999, as a visiting lecturer at the National University of Rwanda, Butare. The last verse came much later as a reflection on the country's national 'justice and reconciliation' process.

Bagamoyo Smile was written after my first visit to Bagamoyo, the historic coastal town in Tanzania at the end of one of the slave routes in East Africa. *'Na wewe, jina lako nani?'* means 'and what is your name?' in Kishwahili.

Salme's Night Flight evokes the well-known story in Zanzibar of Princess Sayyida Salme, daughter of the Sultan, Al-Busaid, who eloped in 1866 with a German trader and became Emily Ruete.

Starehe – Nafsi Poa '*Starehe*' means 'comfort' or 'relaxation' in Kiswahili; it is also the name of a club in Zanzibar. '*Nafsi poa*' is a slang meaning cool soul/person.

Desert Flower was written after an encounter in 2002 at the international airport in Dar es Salaam with a mentally disturbed young woman whom I later discovered, I had taught some years earlier in UK.

One Season Of Voyages is a reflection on ten years living in Tanzania.

Acknowledgements

Thanks are due to the editors of the following publications where some of these poems were previously published – *Ghana Nsem*, *Pambazuka News*, *Wasafiri*, *Fanani Flava* and Neil Astley and Anna Selby (eds) *The World Record*.

'Tears and Laughter Embrace in the Blood-Stained Forest', 'Abstract' and part of 'Tangled Melodies' were first published in *Secret Lives* (Bogle L'Ouverture, 1986).